# Foods of Cuba

## Barbara Sheen

**KIDHAVEN PRESS**
*A part of Gale, Cengage Learning*

 GALE
CENGAGE Learning

Detroit • New York • San Francisco • New Haven, Conn • Waterville, Maine • London

© 2011 Gale, Cengage Learning

| LIBRARY OF CONGRESS CATALOGING-IN-PUBLICATION DATA |
| --- |
| Sheen, Barbara.<br>   Foods of Cuba / by Barbara Sheen.<br>      p. cm. -- (A taste of culture)<br>   Includes bibliographical references and index.<br>   ISBN 978-0-7377-5113-0 (hardcover)<br>   1. Cooking, Cuban--Juvenile literature. 2. Cuba--Social life and customs–Juvenile literature. I. Title.<br>   TX716.C8S54 2010<br>   641.597291–dc22<br>                                                                       2010030795 |

Kidhaven Press
27500 Drake Rd.
Farmington Hills MI 48331


ISBN-13: 978-0-7377-5113-0
ISBN-10: 0-7377-5113-4

Printed in the United States of America
1 2 3 4 5 6 7 14 13 12 11 10

Printed by Bang Printing, Brainerd, MN, 1ˢᵗ Ptg., 11/2010

# Contents

# A Beautiful Land

When European explorer Christopher Columbus landed on the Caribbean island of Cuba in 1492, he described it as "The most beautiful land that human eyes have ever seen."[1] With its white sandy beaches, tall palm trees, crystal clear waters, and tropical climate, Cuba is indeed a beautiful place. Cuban cooking is equally noteworthy. Cuban cooks depend on black beans, rice, garlic, **plantains**, and root vegetables to give their foods a tropical flavor that is as lovely as the island itself.

## Black Beans

Cubans love black beans. They have been eating them for centuries. The beans, which are believed to have originated in Central America, were an important part of the diet of Cuba's earliest inhabitants, the Taino-Arawak Indians.

At any given moment, there is likely to be a pot of black beans cooking in almost every Cuban kitchen. Black beans are an essential side dish to most Cuban meals, and are often a meal on their own. "We can easily eat black beans for breakfast, lunch, and dinner,"[2] explains chef Jorge Castillo.

Every Cuban cook has his or her own recipe for black

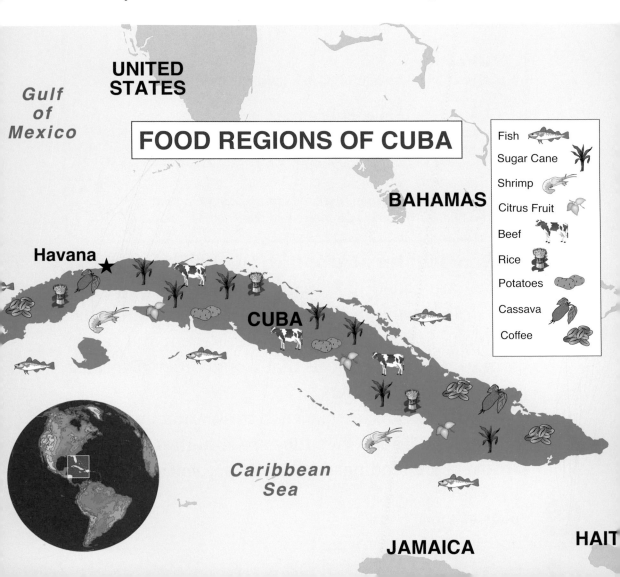

FOOD REGIONS OF CUBA

Fish
Sugar Cane
Shrimp
Citrus Fruit
Beef
Rice
Potatoes
Cassava
Coffee

Gulf of Mexico

UNITED STATES

BAHAMAS

Havana

CUBA

Caribbean Sea

JAMAICA

HAIT

# Black Beans

This recipe starts with sofrito, which is easy to make. This recipe can be made with dried black beans or canned beans, for an easier version.

## Ingredients
1 (15 oz.) can black beans
1 red onion, peeled and chopped
1 green bell pepper, chopped
1 small tomato, chopped
5 cloves garlic, peeled and chopped
3 tablespoons olive oil

## Directions
1. Heat 2 tablespoons of oil in a saucepan over medium-low heat.
2. Make sofrito by adding the garlic, onion, pepper, and tomato, and sauté until the onions are translucent.
3. Add the beans, mix well. Then add 1 tablespoon of olive oil. Cook over low heat, stirring frequently until the beans are hot.

Leftover beef, chicken, pork, or sausage can be added with the beans. The beans can be served over rice. Serves 4.

beans, or **frijoles negros** (free-HOH-lays NAY-grohs), as they are called in Cuba. Traditionally, cooks start with dried beans that they wash carefully then soak overnight. Soaking the beans softens them and causes them to release chemicals that would otherwise cause gas when they are eaten.

Next, the beans are placed in fresh water and boiled for about an hour. Once they are soft, they are left to **simmer**. Depending on the recipe, spices like gar-

*Frijoles negros are a popular Cuban dish. Black beans are cooked with spices and sometimes also with onions and green pepper.*

lic and oregano and vegetables like onions and green pepper are added to the simmering pot. The beans, which are loaded with vitamins, minerals, and protein, have a hearty, rich flavor similar to mushrooms. They are served over rice, mixed with chicken, made into bean salad, or eaten on their own.

They also can be turned into black bean soup, which may be Cuba's most famous dish. To make the soup, Cuban cooks crush the beans. This causes them to burst open and release thick black juice. The juice and crushed beans are topped with a splash of vinegar, a slice of avocado, a spoonful of sour cream, and a sprig of **cilantro** (see-LAHN-tro). The result is a creamy and hearty soup.

## Rice

Black beans are almost always accompanied by, or mixed with, rice, another important staple of the Cuban diet. Rice originated in Asia. Spanish colonists brought it to Cuba in the 16th century. It grew well and became an essential part of nearly every meal. Cubans

## Cuba Today

Up until 1959, when Fidel Castro became the president of Cuba, the United States and Cuba had a close relationship. When Castro took over, however, he set up a Communist government with close ties to the former Soviet Union (USSR). Communism eliminated private ownership of farms and businesses. As a result, many Cubans immigrated to the United States. Today, there are about 1.5 million Cubans living in the United States.

In 1961 the United States banned all trade with Cuba. The Soviet Union became Cuba's main trading partner. Much of what Cubans ate was either grown on government-run farms that depended on Soviet-made fertilizers and farm equipment, or was imported from the Soviet Union. When the Soviet Union collapsed in 1991, Cuba faced food shortages. Castro remained Cuba's president until 2008, when his brother Raul took over.

mix rice with black or red beans. They fry it with pork and vegetables. They turn it into a cold salad, much like American potato salad. They mix it with okra and with all types of seafood. They cook it with coconut milk, sugar, and cream to make arroz con coco (ah-ROHS cohn COH-coh), or coconut rice pudding, a sweet, rich, fragrant, and uniquely Cuban treat.

Not just any rice will do. Cubans prefer long-grain rice, which they cook until it is soft, light, and fluffy. Cuban cooks are often judged on the quality of their rice. "The ability to make perfect white rice is perhaps the most indispensable skill of Cuban cooking," author María Josefa Lluriá de O'Higgins explains. "Cuban rice should neither be mushy nor as the Italians say al dente [firm]. It should be light and airy—never sticky. It is the foundation [beginning] of such a large proportion [number] of Cuba's distinctive dishes that woe to the cook who has not mastered its secret."[3]

And, when Cubans want to add color and exotic flavor to their rice they add a bit of **saffron**, a costly spice that turns the rice bright yellow and gives it a tea-like flavor. Arroz con pollo (ah-ROHS cohn POH-yo),

*Saffron, upper left, is a spice that can be cooked with rice to turn the rice a bright yellow color. The Cuban dish arroz con pollo is often made with saffron rice.*

or chicken with rice, is a popular dish that is seasoned with saffron. So is paella (pah-AY-ya). This elaborate stew-like dish combines rice with peas, onions, garlic, peppers, sausage, ham, chicken, and a wide range of seafood like lobster, shrimp, crabmeat, and clams.

## Garlic

Garlic is a key ingredient in paella and arroz con pollo. In fact, most Cuban cooks would not think of making rice without garlic.

Garlic gives Cuban stews, sauces, seafood, chicken, salads, and soup a savory flavor. Garlic soup is a popu-

# Mojo Sauce

Mojo sauce can be used to marinate chicken, fish, pork, and beef. It can also be poured over steamed vegetables, and is a tasty dipping sauce. It is easy to make. In Cuba, it is made with sour orange juice, which is hard to find in the United States. This recipe uses a sweet orange and lime juice instead.

### Ingredients
½ cup orange juice
½ cup lime juice
6 garlic cloves, peeled and crushed
½ cup extra virgin olive oil
salt to taste

### Directions
1. Put all ingredients into a blender and blend until the mixture is smooth.

Makes 1 cup. Serve as a dip for plantain or other chips.

*A man prepares sofrito in his home. Garlic is an important ingredient in this popular dish.*

lar Cuban mainstay. It is eaten for its good taste and because it is believed to promote good health. Garlic toast also accompanies most meals. According to chef Raul Musibay, "Very few Cuban dishes don't include a healthy dose of garlic. It adds such a great flavor to everything."[4]

Garlic's most important use is in **sofrito** (soh-FREE-toe) and **mojo** (MOH-ho), two concoctions that give Cuban food its distinctive flavor. Sofrito is a zesty mixture made by lightly frying or **sautéing** green peppers, onions, garlic, oregano, bay leaves, and sometimes tomatoes. Cubans use it to season anything and everything. Cuban-born writer Mayra L. Dole explains that sofrito is "our secret ingredient used for cooking black beans, stews, meats, fish, and anything, really. . . . I'm surprised we don't use sofrito in our desserts."[5]

Although many people say sofrito tastes best when it is freshly made, many Cuban cooks premake large batches and then refrigerate them. This is because sofrito is used so often. It is also available ready-made in Cuban grocery stores, much like salsa. Either way, sofrito adds flavor to Cuban foods without adding heat, which is characteristic of Cuban food. It is spiced, but not spicy.

Mojo adds another distinct flavor. This sauce combines garlic and the juice of sour oranges. When it is added to meat and fish, it gives the food a tangy exotic flavor and a citrusy aroma. At the same time the acid in the sour orange juice **tenderizes** meat and fish, making them fork-tender.

# Organic Farming in Cuba

Organic farms are those that do not use chemical fertilizers or pesticides. When the Soviet Union collapsed in 1991, Cuba's large state-run farms were in trouble. They could not run without Soviet farm equipment and Soviet-made fertilizers and pesticides.

Faced with food shortages, Cubans set up small urban farms known as organoponicos in vacant lots, backyards, roof tops, and parking lots. Since chemical fertilizer and pesticides were unavailable, the organoponicos grew organic produce. Instead of tractors, work was done manually or with horses and oxen.

Today, there are more than 200 organoponicos in Havana alone. They produce tons of fresh produce each year. In fact, Cuba has become a model of semi-sustainable farming. This type of farming does not depend on chemicals, oil, or foreign trade. Cuba's organoponicos have won international awards.

*Farmers work on an organoponico in Havana. Cuba's capital city contains more than 200 organic farms.*

# Exotic Starchy Vegetables and Fruit

Starchy root vegetables like **yuca** (YOO-cah), **boniatos** (boh-nee-AH-toes), and **malangas** (mah-LAHN-gahs) add more exotic flavors to Cuban meals, so do plantains, a starchy tropical fruit. Yuca, which is native to Cuba, was a staple of the Taino-Arawak Indians' diet. It is very tough until it is boiled, then it becomes soft and tender. It tastes similar to a potato. Yuca con mojo, which is yuca marinated in mojo sauce, is a popular Cuban dish.

Malangas can also be boiled and served in mojo sauce. Malangas taste similar to yams. They have a shaggy brown skin that resembles that of a coconut, with either a white or a yellow interior. Boniatos look like white potatoes, but they have a sweeter more delicate taste. They taste like a cross between white and sweet potatoes. Cubans use them in stews and desserts, and they fry them like french fries.

Plantains also are fried. Plantains look like large green ba-

*Plantains look like large green bananas and are often fried into chips. When cooked, they can taste a bit sweet.*

nanas, but they are too hard and bitter to eat raw. When fried, mashed, or boiled, they taste similar to potatoes.

If plantains are left to ripen, they turn black on the outside and become as sweet as candy. Baked ripe plantains topped with butter, brown sugar, and cinnamon make a delicious tropical dessert, especially when they are served with vanilla ice cream.

Plantains, starchy root vegetables, rice, black beans, garlic, and Cuban sauces like mojo and sofrito give Cuban cooking its exotic flavor. These ingredients are as unique, rich, and flavorful as the island itself.

# A Cultural Stew

**M**any different groups have played a role in shaping Cuba's history. The Taino-Arawak Indians were Cuba's earliest inhabitants. They arrived around 1050 AD. When Christopher Columbus reached Cuba in 1492, he claimed the island for Spain. Spanish settlers arrived shortly thereafter. They brought African slaves and Chinese **indentured servants** to work on the sugar plantations they established. With the help of American troops, Cuba gained its independence from Spain in 1898 in a war known as the Spanish-American War. As an independent nation, it developed strong ties to the United States, but political differences ended relations between the two countries in 1959.

All of these groups influenced Cuban culture. The

# Many Backgrounds

Not all Cubans are of Spanish, African, or Native Indian descent. There are many Cubans of French, British, Polish, German, Russian, Italian, Greek, Turkish, Syrian, and Jewish descent.

There are also many Chinese Cubans. They are the descendants of indentured servants who worked on Cuban sugar plantations. Once they had fulfilled the terms of their contracts many moved to Havana, where they opened small businesses and restaurants. At one time, Havana had the largest Chinese population in Latin America.

Most of the Chinese settled in the same part of Havana, which became known as Chinatown. Here, street and shop signs were written in Spanish and Chinese. Havana's Chinatown also had its own Chinese newspapers.

After Castro took power, many Chinese Cubans left Cuba. But there are still many Chinese Cubans living in Havana today.

*Cuba contains people from diverse backgrounds, including Spanish, African, German, Italian, and Jewish.*

*A model of Taino-Arawak Indians is displayed in a reproduction of their village. The Taino-Arawak Indians were one of Cuba's earliest inhabitants.*

Cuban people's favorite dishes reflect the cooking styles and ingredients these cultural groups brought to the island, combined with the tropical flavor that is characteristic of Cuba.

## Cuba's National Dish

**Ajiaco** (AH-hee-AH-coh), a hearty stew, is Cuba's national dish. Like the island itself, it represents a blending of many cultures.

The Taino-Arawak Indians were the first to make ajiaco. Their version featured native root vegetables and

## Fish and Seafood

Although Cuba is an island, in the past poor roads and lack of refrigeration made it difficult for Cubans who lived inland to get fresh seafood.

Fresh fish and other seafood, however, were accessible to Cubans living on the coast. Many owned boats from which they caught swordfish, lobster, crab, shrimp, and squid, among other water creatures. Those without boats had an interesting way of catching fish. They attached their bait, hook, and line to a kite. The kite carried the bait far from the shore where there were more fish. In this manner, they were able to catch fish like red snapper, blue snapper, grouper, cod, and black mullet.

plantains flavored with bits of dried goat meat. Since Cuba's warm climate caused meat to spoil easily, the Indians developed a way to preserve meat by rubbing it with salt and spices then drying it in the sun.

When the Spanish arrived they brought cattle, pigs, sheep, and chickens, as well as garlic, sugar, and rice with them. The Spanish colonists adopted the Indians' method of preserving meat. It was not long before **tasajo** (tah-SAH-ho), salt-dried beef, found its way into ajiaco. It is similar to beef jerky, but when it is soaked in liquid, it becomes soft and tender.

Many of the Spanish settlers had African slaves who cooked meals for them. These Africans added spices like cumin and black pepper and produce like pumpkin and tomatoes to the stew.

Ajiaco, a stew, is Cuba's national dish. The recipe has been changed by all of Cuba's inhabitants who arrived from other places.

Today there are probably as many ways to make ajiaco as there are Cuban cooks. With the exception of native root vegetables, there are no set ingredients. Most cooks start with sofrito. They may add chicken, tasajo, steak or brisket, pork, corn, pumpkin, plantains, malangas, bonitos, yuca, garlic, and tomatoes to the pot, depending on their taste and what they have on hand.

No matter the exact ingredients, ajiaco is always cooked slowly so that all the flavors meld, or combine. It may be cooked on the stove, in a slow cooker, or a pressure cooker. When it is so thick and rich that it must be eaten with a fork, it is ready to eat.

Served in a bowl topped with a squirt of lemon or lime juice and a hunk of soft Cuban bread, ajiaco is hearty, healthy, and delicious. O'Higgins, calls it "a meal in itself."[6]

The use of so many native plants in the stew makes it uniquely Cuban. In fact, in the 1930s Cuba's president ordered all Cubans to eat the tasty stew once a week so that Cuba would lessen its growing dependence on imported processed foods from the United States.

## Old Clothes

**Ropa vieja** (ROH-pah vee-AY-hah), which means "old clothes," is another very popular Cuban stew. It has its roots in the Canary Islands, which are located off the coast of Spain. Many of Cuba's earliest Spanish settlers came from the Canary Islands.

The dish combines sofrito, tomatoes, and beef. It

*The popular stew ropa vieja is made with shredded meat, sofrito, and tomatoes. It is cooked very slowly.*

probably got its name because the meat in the stew is first browned and then cooked slowly until it is so tender that it shreds into thin strips that look like frayed bits of cloth. Val Prieto, founding editor of Babalu, a Web site dedicated to Cuba, recalls, "My mom would make it at least once a week and my sister and I would drive her crazy saying old clothes, old clothes, old clothes. We're eating old clothes."[7]

Out of necessity, Cuba's slave population perfected this type of slow cooking. They typically were given the toughest cuts of meat for their food. Slow cooking turns even the toughest meat fork tender.

# Avocado Salad

Avocados grow well in Cuba. Avocado salad is a popular side dish. The salad should be eaten right away because avocado slices blacken when exposed to air.

## Ingredients
4 small avocados
⅓ cup small sweet onion, peeled and sliced
1 small head Boston (butter) lettuce (iceberg lettuce can be substituted), washed
1 tablespoon extra virgin olive oil
1 teaspoon lime juice
salt and pepper to taste

## Directions
1. Arrange lettuce leaves on a platter.
2. Slice the avocado into bite-size chunks. Put them on top of the lettuce leaves.
3. Add the onion slices.
4. Mix the oil, lime juice, salt, and pepper together. Pour over the salad.

Serves 4.

*Avocados are a key ingredient in a popular salad side dish.*

The tender meat usually is accompanied by plain white rice. Cubans learned to feature rice as a side dish from the Chinese. Before their arrival, Cubans cooked with rice, but they rarely served it as a side dish.

The combination of the melt-in-the-mouth tender meat, sweet tomatoes, zesty sofrito, and delicate rice makes ropa vieja delicious. It is believed to taste even better reheated the next day when the flavors have had even more time to blend together. It is, according to Prieto, "one of Cuba's quintessential culinary [classic cooking] delights."[8]

## Moros y Cristianos

**Moros y Cristianos** (MOR-ohs ee CREE-stee-AH-nohs), which means "Moors and Christians," is another favorite Cuban dish with a rich background. In fact, it gets its name from events in Spanish history.

The Moors were North Africans who invaded Spain in the 8th century and occupied the country from 711 until 1492 AD. They had a lasting impact on Spanish culture. The dish, which was invented by Cuba's earliest Spanish settlers, features black beans, which represent the Moors, and white rice, which represents the Spanish. But, unlike other beans-and-rice dishes in which the beans are served over rice, in Moros y Cristianos the beans and rice are cooked together. This allows the flavors to truly mix the same way that African, native, and Spanish cultures blended in Cuba, creating what chef Raul Musibay calls "a perfect example of Cuban unity."[9]

*The Moors, at left, face Spain's king and queen, Ferdinand and Isabella. The Moorish influence in Spain made its way to Cuba with Spanish settlers.*

To make Moros y Cristianos, cooks first make sofrito and add bacon to it. At the same time, they cook the beans. When the beans are tender, the sofrito and uncooked rice are added to the pot and the mixture is cooked until the rice is soft and fluffy. The finished dish is topped with a splash of olive oil and a sprig of cilantro. It tastes warm, rich, and creamy.

## Tropical Hash

**Picadillo** (PEE-cah-DEE-yo) is another popular dish. It is Cuban-style hash or minced meat. In fact, the word picadillo means "small bits and pieces." The dish was brought to Spain by the Moors, and eventually made its way to Cuba.

# Picadillo

There are many different ways to make picadillo. Some cooks like to add fried potatoes. Some like to top each serving with a fried egg. Some use fresh tomatoes rather than tomato sauce. Picadillo can also be made with chunks of cooked white fish rather than ground beef.

## Ingredients
1 red onion, peeled and chopped
1 green pepper, chopped
4 garlic cloves, chopped
1 pound ground beef
1 small can (7–8 oz.) tomato sauce
2 tablespoons olive oil
¼ cup raisins
¼ cup pimento stuffed green olives, chopped
⅛ teaspoon cinnamon
⅛ teaspoon oregano

## Directions
1. Heat the oil in a large pan over medium heat. Add the garlic, onion, and pepper and cook until the onion is translucent.
2. Add the meat, stirring to break it up.
3. Add all the other ingredients. Reduce the heat to low. Cover the pot. Cook until the meat is browned throughout. Stir occasionally.

Serves 4. Serve over rice or Cuban bread.

It is one of the Cuban people's favorite meals because it is tasty, easy to make, and can include a wide range of ingredients, which makes it a good way to use leftovers. Chef Glenn Lindgren, who is married to a Cu-

*Picadillo is a Cuban-style hash that originated from the Moors. It can include a lot of different ingredients and is often served with fried plantains.*

ban American, says, "In a Cuban household picadillo is the equivalent of several American home-style favorites: sloppy Joes, Hamburger Helper and homemade spaghetti—all things that a mom can prepare simply and inexpensively for her family."[10]

Picadillo mixes sweet and savory flavors, a characteristic of North African cooking. Cuban picadillo combines ground beef, sofrito, tomatoes, green olives, cinnamon, cloves, and raisins. Some cooks add fried potatoes, an American touch. Many top the dish with a fried egg.

Picadillo looks similar to sloppy Joes, but its sweet, sour, and salty taste is quite different. Cuban cooks usually serve it over hot white rice. Fried plantains, which taste similar to french fries, are a typical tropical accompaniment.

For Cubans, picadillo is a taste of home. Marta Darby, who emigrated from Cuba to the United States, recalls, "When we were new to this country, my mom experimented with all kinds of traditional, inexpensive American foods. ...My dad . . . got very vocal about getting his picadillo at least once a week. The moment we smelled the sofrito, all was right again in our little exile world. . . . Picadillo . . . is my absolute favorite comfort food."[11]

The Cuban people's favorite dishes are comforting, hearty, exotic, and delicious. Like the nation itself, Cuban cooking reflects a blend of the many cultures that are a part of its history. Cuban cooks have added their own touches to make these dishes their own.

# Chapter 3

# Snacks and Treats

**C**ubans like to snack. Vendors selling savory and sweet treats from street stalls, baskets, and wheelbarrows are a common sight on the streets of Havana, Cuba's capital. Delicious smells fill the air, tempting passersby to stop and have a bite to eat.

## Fried Treats

Many of the Cuban people's favorite snacks are fried, which makes them crunchy. **Marquitas** (mar-KEE-tahs) and **tostones** (toh-STOH-nays) are among the most popular. Marquitas look and taste like potato chips, but they are actually salted, deep-fried plantain chips. They are sold pre-made in grocery stores, as well as hot and fresh in little cafés, fine restaurants, and in

30

*A tasty snack, tostones are twice-fried plaintain chips. They can be shaped into little cups and filled with meat or seafood.*

street stalls. They are eaten not only in Cuba, but also in the Caribbean island nations of Puerto Rico and the Dominican Republic. According to author Viviana Carballo, who was born and raised in Havana, "Universal in the Spanish-speaking Caribbean, plantain chips are claimed as their own by each and every single island. They've spread all over and you are as likely to find them in chic establishments as in the corner bodega [grocery store]. The truth is there couldn't be a simpler and tastier alternative to potato chips."[12]

Tostones also are plantain chips that are fried twice, making them extra crispy. This method of double-frying came to Cuba with the African slaves who double-fried plantains in this way in the Congo.

To make tostones, plantains cut into 1 inch (2.54cm) rounds are fried in hot oil. The oil temperature is very important. It must be about 360°F (182°C). If it is too hot, the tostones will burn. If it is not hot enough, they become soggy. But when the oil temperature is just

# Marquitas

Marquitas are similar to potato chips, but they are made with plantains. Plantains are sold in most supermarkets. They can be difficult to peel, especially if they are stored in the refrigerator. It is best to warm a plantain to room temperature before peeling.

### Ingredients
1 green plantain
½ cup corn or safflower oil
salt to taste

### Directions
1. Peel the plantain. Cut off the ends and slit the plantain lengthwise. The slit should be as deep as the peel. Using a short knife for help, remove the peel starting at the slit. The peel should come off in four sections.
2. Cut the peeled plantain into thin rounds.
3. Heat the oil in the pan over medium heat. When the oil is hot (about 360°F [182°C]) add the plantain rounds. Fry until the rounds are brown on both sides.
4. Put the marquitas in a paper bag, sprinkle with salt, and shake the bag.

Serve marquitas hot.
Serves 2.

right, the tostones cook perfectly.

The tostones are fried until they start turning brown. Then, they are drained and put in a tostonera (toh-stow-NAIR-ah), a pressing device made of two pieces of hinged wood, metal, or plastic, which flattens the tostones and shapes them into small patties. The patties are returned to the hot oil and refried. When the tostones are hot and golden, they are put in a paper bag with a sprinkle of salt. The cook shakes the bag, which allows some of the oil to be blotted up by the paper while lightly salting the tostones.

Or, the tostones may be shaped into little cups. Some tostoneras are made to do this. Cooks fill the

## Guarapa

Sugarcane juice, or guarapa (guah-RAH-pa), is a popular Cuban drink. To make guarapa, peeled sugarcane is put in a guarapa press, a contraption that crushes the sugarcane and squeezes out the juice. The press looks like a big box. It has a hole in the front that the sugarcane is fed into. A device inside extracts the juice, which comes out through a hole in the press. A container is placed by the hole to catch the juice. Surprisingly, the juice is not extremely sweet. It is slightly sweeter than orange juice and has a light, refreshing taste. It is usually served with a squeeze of lime.

*A glass of sugar cane juice sits next to sugar cane sticks.*

cup-shaped tostones with seafood, pork, or chicken. According to Haley Suzanne, the author of the cooking blog Appoggiatura, tostones are "salty, chewy, melty, tangy, crunchy. . . . So many good flavors."[13]

## Tasty Fritters

Croquetas (croh-KAY-tahs) are still another favorite fried snack. Croquetas are fritters, or croquettes, made with a wide variety of ingredients. There are beef fritters, ham fritters, fish fritters, and chicken fritters, just to name a few. To make fritters, cooks shred or grind the main ingredient and mix it with flour, milk, onions, and butter.

Next, the mixture is shaped into little logs. These are rolled in a combination of breadcrumbs and eggs and fried in hot oil until the outside is crisp and golden and the inside is moist and tender. Cubans gobble them down right out of the pan. Enrique Fernandez, who was born and raised in Cuba, explains that his sons, "would eat 10 at a time each, then pack more for the road. . . . I, too, have been hooked on croquetas since childhood, when they were my snackbar lunch every noon one summer after swimming lessons at a Havana pool."[14]

## A Cuban Sandwich

Grilled sandwiches are another favorite Cuban snack. One known as a Cuban sandwich is far and away the most popular. No one knows where or when it originated. Historians think it was created in the early 20th century by vendors who sold quick meals to Cuban sugar mill and cigar factory workers.

The hearty sandwich starts with Cuban bread, which looks similar to French bread but is sweeter tasting and has a softer texture. The bread is sliced and spread with butter. Roast pork, ham, Swiss cheese, and pickles are layered between the bread. Then, the sandwich is grilled in a plancha (PLAHN-cha), a sandwich press similar to a waffle iron. Or, it is cooked in a pan while

*The most popular grilled sandwich in Cuba is called a Cuban sandwich. A lighter version of the sandwich is called medianoche.*

# Cuban Sandwich

A medianoche, or Cuban sandwich, is easy to make. To prepare one use a small, soft roll instead of bread. For a heartier sandwich add more meat and cheese. The sandwich can be heated in a frying pan, panini press, or on a griddle.

## Ingredients
One 8-inch section of Cuban or French bread, sliced lengthwise
1 slice roast pork
1 slice ham
1 slice Swiss cheese
1 small dill pickle, sliced
butter or margarine, softened

## Directions
1. Coat the frying pan with nonstick spray, then preheat it on low.
2. Spread both halves of the bread with butter or margarine. Add the pickles, pork, ham, and cheese.
3. Put the sandwich in the pan. Put a heavy plate or skillet on top of it and press down hard. Keep pressing as the sandwich grills.
4. When the bottom layer of bread is lightly toasted (about 2 minutes) turn the sandwich over, and repeat the pressing. The sandwich is done when the cheese is melted and both bread halves are toasted.

Makes one sandwich.

the cook presses a heavy skillet on top of the sandwich. The heat and the pressure cause the cheese to melt, the meats and pickles to release their juices, and the bread to develop a crunchy crust.

And for those who have a smaller appetite, there is the medianoche (MAY-dee-ah-NO-chay). It is a lighter version of the Cuban sandwich, made on a small sweet torpedo-shaped roll. In fact, the sandwich got its name, medianoche, which means "midnight," because it is such a popular late-night treat. Tiny versions of the sandwich, known as bocaditos (boh-cah-DEE-toes) or little mouthfuls are served at parties much like **hors d'oeuvres** (or-DERVS). These are made on bite-sized round rolls.

Large or small, a Cuban sandwich is hard to resist. Ron Witt, an American who was stationed at the U.S. naval base in Guantánamo, Cuba, recalls, "We used to venture off limits to the Cuban Village to buy the Cuban sandwiches. . . . The sandwiches were cooked in a sandwich press, like we use to make grilled cheese sandwiches. They were placed four at a time in the press and then it was closed. . . . After a few minutes they were done, golden brown. They were then wrapped in tin foil and placed in a paper bag. . . . We never ever tasted anything so delicious."[15]

## Strong Coffee

Cuban sandwiches, croquetas, tostones, and other snacks are almost always washed down with a cafecito (cah-fay-CEE-toe), strong Cuban coffee similar to espresso. Cafecito is often a snack on its own.

Cafecito is brewed in an electric espresso machine. The coffee drips into a small pot containing at least one teaspoon of sugar for each cup. Since cafecito is served in tiny cups, even a small amount of sugar makes the drink very sweet. As soon as the coffee starts dripping into the sugar-laden pot, the coffee is stirred briskly. This causes creamy foam known as espumita (es-pooh-MEE-tah) to form. The foam rises to the top when cafecito is poured into a cup.

Cubans usually do not add milk to cafecito. They like it dark and sweet. Most Cubans drink it at least once a day. They say it gives them energy.

Having a cafecito with friends is a popular social event, and cafecito breaks at work are common. Ac-

## Tropical Fruit Batidos

Batidos, or smoothies, are popular Cuban snacks. They are made with fruit, milk, ice, and sugar. What makes them special are the tropical fruits they feature. Some popular flavors include papaya, mango, mamey, and passion fruit.

Cuban papayas can be as large as watermelons. They have a greenish yellow skin and a sweet pink interior. Papayas have a pleasant taste, and are believed to aid digestion.

Mangos are extremely juicy fruits. They have a rich fruity aroma, green skin, and a sweet yellow interior with a large black pit in the middle of the fruit.

Mameys can be as small as a peach or as big as a cantaloupe. Their skin is fuzzy and feels like sandpaper, but their orange flesh is smooth and creamy. The flesh of a passion fruit, on the other hand, is like jelly. It has a slightly tart taste and an incredibly fragrant aroma.

cording to Mayra Dole, "Break time for every Cuban on Earth—I don't care if you live in a cave or the North Pole—is the time for a cafecito. . . . We drink lots of cafecitos. Café is in our blood and bones."[16]

Cafecito is sold in cafés and restaurants, and at walk-up windows. Besides being served with savory snacks, it often accompanies flaky little puff pastries known as **pastelitos** (pah-stay-LEE-toes) filled with a paste made of guava. Guava is a fragrant tropical fruit about the size of a plum. Green on the outside and red on the inside, guavas are very juicy and sweet. Guava paste, which combines the fruit with sugar, is even sweeter. Although, non-Cubans may find guava pastelitos too sweet for their taste, most Cubans love them. Says Carballo, "I find them irresistible."[17]

Indeed, snacks like cafecito, pastelitos, marquitas, tostones, croquetas, and medianoches are hard to resist. With choices like these, it is no surprise that Cubans love to snack.

# chapter
# 4

# Time to Celebrate

Cubans enjoy getting together with family and friends. Almost any occasion is a chance to have a party. Food plays a big part in every Cuban celebration. "The perfect Cuban party includes these things: good food, good friends, good music, more good food,"[18] explains Raul Musibay.

## Noche Buena Festivities

Christmas Eve, or **Noche Buena** (NO-chay BWAY-nah), as it is known in Cuba, is the most festive occasion of the year. It is common for dozens of guests to attend Noche Buena celebrations, and for mountains of food to be served. Cubans are known for their hospitality. Friends, family, neighbors, and acquaintances

*Lechon asado, at upper right, is served here with onions, black beans, and fried plantains. The dish is traditionally eaten on Christmas Eve.*

are all welcome. Often guests go from house to house, attending one Noche Buena celebration after another.

Preparations for making **lechon asado** (LAY-chohn ah-SAH-doh), a whole roasted young pig, begin on December 23rd. It is the main dish at the celebration. A young pig is used because its meat is more tender than that of an older pig. Readying the pig for cooking, as well as actually cooking it, is the job of the man of the house. In the past, he had to kill the animal, split it open, remove the internal organs, and clean off the

# Quinceañeras

A quinceañera (KEEN-say-ahn-YAIR-ah) is a big party that honors a girl's passage from childhood to womanhood on her fifteenth birthday.

The event starts with the birthday girl receiving a blessing in church. She then makes a grand entrance at the party, where her guests and her royal court await her. The royal court consists of fourteen pairs. Each represents a year of the honoree's life.

The birthday girl has her first dance with her father. He then passes her on to other male family members and finally to her escort. Many girls take dancing lessons in preparation.

There is lots of food and a spectacular multitiered birthday cake with fifteen candles each dedicated to an important person in the birthday girl's life. She makes a speech about each person as the candles are lit.

*A girl is escorted by young men at her quinceañera.*

hair and bristles before the cooking could begin. Modern Cubans are more likely to start with an oven-ready pig that they buy from a butcher.

Even with an oven-ready pig, there is still much to do. The pig is carefully rubbed with mojo inside and out. Then, it is refrigerated overnight so it can absorb the tangy sauce, which tenderizes it and adds zesty flavor.

Cooking starts early the next morning. Traditionally, the pig is roasted on a grill over a pit lined with guava leaves and branches. The pig is covered with plantain leaves, which keeps it from drying out. This tradition began before Cubans had modern ovens. As with American barbecuing, it is still popular today.

Roasting is an all-day affair. Depending on the pig's size, it can take from four to eight hours to cook it. Usually all the men in the family, as well as male friends and neighbors, gather around the pit to watch the fire and **baste** the pig with mojo as it cooks. Once the pig is done on one side, they turn it over. This gathering is actually the start of the party since the men snack, drink, and visit throughout the day. Jokingly, Musibay calls this "the 'hard' part, sitting around, drinking beer, telling jokes, enjoying the sunshine, and oh yeah, watching the pig roast."[19]

The lechon is done when the skin is crispy and the meat is so moist and tender that it is falling off the bone. It is usually served with black beans, rice, tostones, yuca cooked in mojo sauce, an avocado salad, and Cuban bread. The festivities often go on until midnight when everyone heads to church.

## Delicious Desserts

The Noche Buena party is not over without dessert. Most Cubans love sweets. Usually trays filled with different sweets are served. Bunuelos (boon-WAY-los)

*Bunuelos are fried pastries that are such a part of Noche Buena that they are mentioned in a song.*

and torticas de Navidad (tor-TEE-cahs day NAH-bee-dahd) are sure to be included.

Like all Cuban pastries, both are very sweet. Sugarcane is grown on the island. In fact, in the past Cuba was known as the world's sugar bowl. Cuban bakers take advantage of the abundance of sugar in their creations.

Bunuelos are fried pastries that are made with a combination of yuca and malanga mixed into the dough. They are formed into a figure eight and fried until they are golden brown. Crisp on the outside and moist on the inside, bunuelos are drenched in sweet syrup made with sugar, water, lemon peel, cinnamon, and anise powder. Anise is an herb with a licorice flavor.

Bunuelos are so connected to Noche Buena that a traditional Cuban Christmas carol begins, "Tonight is Christmas Eve, a night to eat bunuelos."[20]

## Cornflakes, Nuts, and Fruit

Torticas de Navidad, or Cuban Christmas cookies, are also closely linked to Christmas Eve. They are made with cornflakes. Americans, who helped set up factories and businesses in Cuba in the 1940s and 1950s, introduced the breakfast cereal to Cuba. Innovative Cuban bakers added the crunchy cereal to their Christmas cookie recipe.

Torticas de Navidad are made with sweet dough that contains raisins, walnuts or pecans, and maraschino cherries, which are cherries preserved in syrup.

The dough is shaped into little balls and rolled

# Torticas de Navidad

Cuban Christmas cookies are simple to make.

## Ingredients
1 cup butter
½ cup sugar
1 cup flour
1 cup cornflakes, crushed (not crumbs)
1 teaspoon baking soda
½ teaspoon baking powder
1 teaspoon salt
½ cup chopped walnuts
1 cup raisins
¼ cup chopped maraschino cherries
12 whole maraschino cherries

## Directions
1. Preheat the oven to 375°F.
2. Mix the butter and sugar together.
3. Mix the flour, baking soda, baking powder, and salt together. Add flour mixture to the butter mixture. Mix well.
4. Add the chopped cherries, raisins, and nuts. Gently mix.
5. Put the cornflakes in a bowl. Roll a teaspoon of dough into a ball and roll the ball in the cornflakes. Put the ball on a cookie sheet sprayed with nonstick cooking spray. Flatten out the ball. Put a cherry in the middle. Repeat with all the dough.
6. Bake for 10–15 minutes.
Makes about 12 cookies.
Serves 4.

in crushed cornflakes. Then, a maraschino cherry is placed in the center of each cookie and the cookies are baked in the oven. The cookies are colorful, sugary, chewy, and crunchy. Many cooks make dozens at a time because they are so popular.

## More Festive Desserts

Other festive desserts such as **flan** (flahn) and **tres leches** (trace LAY-chays) **cake** are likely to be served, too. They are favorites not only at Christmas but other occasions as well.

Rich, satiny flan is a custard dish that was brought to Cuba by early Spanish settlers. To prepare it, cooks first make caramel syrup of sugar and water. A mixture of eggs, sugar, and milk is poured over the syrup. The flan is then transferred into individual custard cups that are placed in a water bath, a larger pan filled with hot water.

The whole thing goes in the oven. As the flan bakes, the water distributes the oven's heat. This allows the

## Cuban Wedding Cakes

Cuban brides do not throw their bouquets to unmarried female wedding guests the way American brides do. Instead, Cuban wedding cakes contain a surprise. Ribbons, whose ends hang out of the cake, are baked inside of the cake. A ring, which is hidden inside the cake, is attached to one ribbon. Before the cake is cut, all the single women at the wedding pull a ribbon from the cake. The woman who gets the ribbon with the ring on it is believed to be the next one to get married.

The custard dish flan was brought to Cuba by the Spanish. The sweet dessert is made with eggs, sugar, and milk.

flan to cook slowly without burning, hardening, or becoming crunchy.

The flan is done when it is light, smooth, and creamy. After it cools, the custard cups are turned upside down. As the flan is released, the caramel sauce runs over it, bathing it in sticky sweetness.

Cuban cooks like to give flan a tropical touch by adding shredded coconut or pumpkin to the recipe. The results are exotic and fragrant. "Nothing was better than my madrina's [godmother's] coconut flan," Viviana Carballo recalls. "She made it for me with love."[21]

## Milky Cake

Tres leches, or three-milk, cake is equally delicious. It is served at birthday parties, special family get-togethers, anniversary parties, or any time Cubans want to celebrate. Festive events are incomplete without it.

This sweet, buttery sponge cake originated in Central America, but Cubans adopted it as their own many years ago. The cake gets its name from the three milk products—sweetened condensed milk, evaporated milk, and either cream or coconut milk—that the cake is drenched in. The milk makes the cake incredibly moist, so moist that it can be eaten with a spoon.

To make tres leches cake, cooks bake or buy a sponge cake. They poke small holes all over the cake with a fork and pour the three different types of milk over it. Some cooks add caramel sauce made from cream, sugar, and corn syrup, too. The cake absorbs the different milk flavors without getting mushy. It is refrigerated for a few

# Tres Leches Cake

Tres leches cake can be made from scratch or a yellow cake mix may be used. When time is limited, a store-bought sponge or pound cake can substitute.

## Ingredients
1 yellow cake mix
6 ounces sweetened condensed milk
6 ounces evaporated milk
1 cup whole milk or cream
whipped cream
1 banana

## Directions
1. Prepare and bake the cake following the package directions.
2. Let the cake cool. Put it on a pan with a raised edge so the milk will not spill out. Using a fork, pierce the cake in multiple places on the top and sides.
3. Mix the three milks together. Slowly pour the mixture over the cake, letting it soak in as you pour.

hours, then it is covered with a thick layer of whipped cream and, sometimes, slices of mango or bananas.

The cake is beautiful to look at, and tastes even better. Food writer Mary Luz Meija, describes it as a "spongy, delectable cake, oozing sweet, wonderful milk."[22]

Delectable cakes, sugar-laden pastries, rich and creamy flan, and a pig roasting on a grill mean it is party time in Cuba. Add in friends, family, and neigh-

4. Cover the cake with aluminum foil and refrigerate for at least 2 hours.
5. Thickly spread the whipped cream over the top of the cake. Slice the banana into thin rounds. Use them to decorate the top of the cake.

Makes one cake. Serves 8–12. Keep the cake refrigerated at all times to avoid spoiling.

*Tres leches cake is made with three types of dairy ingredients: condensed milk, evaporated milk, and whole milk. Most are topped with whipped cream while this one is covered with chocolate.*

bors, and Cubans have a recipe for fun. It is no wonder that Cubans love to get together and celebrate. Special foods help make every event more memorable.

# Metric Conversions

## Mass (weight)

| | |
|---|---|
| 1 ounce (oz.) | = 28.0 grams (g) |
| 8 ounces | = 227.0 grams |
| 1 pound (lb.) or 16 ounces | = 0.45 kilograms (kg) |
| 2.2 pounds | = 1.0 kilogram |

## Liquid Volume

| | |
|---|---|
| 1 teaspoon (tsp.) | = 5.0 milliliters (ml) |
| 1 tablespoon (tbsp.) | = 15.0 milliliters |
| 1 fluid ounce (oz.) | = 30.0 milliliters |
| 1 cup (c.) | = 240 milliliters |
| 1 pint (pt.) | = 480 milliliters |
| 1 quart (qt.) | = 0.96 liters (l) |
| 1 gallon (gal.) | = 3.84 liters |

## Pan Sizes

| | |
|---|---|
| 8-inch cake pan | = 20 x 4-centimeter cake pan |
| 9-inch cake pan | = 23 x 3.5-centimeter cake pan |
| 11 x 7-inch baking pan | = 28 x 18-centimeter baking pan |
| 13 x 9-inch baking pan | = 32.5 x 23-centimeter baking pan |
| 9 x 5-inch loaf pan | = 23 x 13-centimeter loaf pan |
| 2-quart casserole | = 2-liter casserole |

## Temperature

| | |
|---|---|
| 212°F | = 100°C (boiling point of water) |
| 225°F | = 110°C |
| 250°F | = 120°C |
| 275°F | = 135°C |
| 300°F | = 150°C |
| 325°F | = 160°C |
| 350°F | = 180°C |
| 375°F | = 190°C |
| 400°F | = 200°C |

## Length

| | |
|---|---|
| 1/4 inch (in.) | = 0.6 centimeters (cm) |
| 1/2 inch | = 1.25 centimeters |
| 1 inch | = 2.5 centimeters |

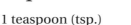

# Notes

## Chapter 1: A Beautiful Land

1. "Cuba: The Most Beautiful Land That Human Eyes Have Ever Seen," *Cuba Journal*, September 10, 2007. http://cubajournal.blogspot .com/2007/09/cuba-most-beautiful-land-that-human.html.

2. Quoted in Glenn Lindgren, Raul Musibay, Jorge Castillo, *Three Guys from Miami Celebrate Cuban.* Salt Lake City: Gibbs Smith, 2006, p. 196.

3. María Josefa Lluriá de O'Higgins, *A Taste of Old Cuba.* New York: HarperCollins, 1994, p. 145.

4. Quoted in Lindgren, Musibay, Castillo, *Three Guys from Miami Celebrate Cuban*, p. 164.

5. Mayra L. Dole, "Cuban Food and Cooking," Inmamaskitchen.com. www.inmamaskitchen.com/FOOD_IS_ART_II/food _history-and-facts/cuban_food_cooking.html.

## Chapter 2: A Cultural Stew

6. O'Higgins, *A Taste of Old Cuba*, p. 25.

7. Val Prieto, "Ropa Vieja," Babalu, March 16, 2006.

8. Prieto, "Ropa Vieja."

9. Quoted in Lindgren, Musibay, Castillo, *Three Guys from Miami Celebrate Cuban*, p. 180.

10. Quoted in Lindgren, Musibay, Castillo, *Three Guys from Miami Celebrate Cuban*, p. 124.

11. Marta Darby, "Comfort Food—From Marta's Cuban American Kitchen." Babalu, March 8, 2007.

## Chapter 3: Snacks and Treats

12. Viviana Carballo, *Havana Salsa.* New York: Atria Books, 2006, p. 81.

13. Haley Suzanne, "Tostones (Fried Green Plantains)."Appoggiatura, July 17, 2009. http://haleysuzanne.wordpress.com/2009/07/17/tostones-fried-green-plantains.

14. Enrique Fernandez, "Croqueticas and Cafecitos 101." Babalu, March 17, 2005.

15. Quoted in "History of Cuban Sandwich, Cubano Sandwich." What's Cooking America. http://whatscookingamerica.net/History/Sandwiches/CubanSandwich.htm.

16. Dole, "Cuban Food and Cooking."

17. Carballo, *Havana Salsa*, p. 71.

## Chapter 4: Time to Celebrate

18. Quoted in Lindgren, Musibay, Castillo, *Three Guys from Miami Celebrate Cuban*, p. 36.

19. Quoted in "How We Roast Pigs." Cuban-Christmas. http://Cuban-christmas.com/pigroast.html.

20. O' Higgins, *A Taste of Old Cuba*, p. 243.

21. Carballo, *Havana Salsa*, p. 57.

22. Mary Luz Meija, "Best Tres Leche Cake Recipe." June 18, 2007. Suite 101. http://cookingresources.suite101.com/article.cfm/best_tres_leches_cake_recipe.

# Glossary

**ajiaco:** A stew that features root vegetables.

**baste:** To use liquid to moisten food.

**boniatos:** Root vegetables that taste like a cross between a potato and a yam.

**cilantro:** An herb, also known as coriander.

**flan:** A custard dessert.

**frijoles negros:** Black beans.

**hors d'oeuvres:** Little appetizers that are served before a meal.

**indentured servants:** Immigrants who work as an unpaid servant for a set number of years in exchange for transportation, food, clothing, and shelter.

**lechon asado:** A roasted young pig.

**malangas:** Root vegetables similar to a sweet potato.

**marquitas:** Fried plantain chips.

**mojo:** A popular sauce made with sour oranges and garlic.

**Moros y Cristianos:** A dish made of black beans and rice.

**Noche Buena:** Christmas Eve.

**pastelitos:** Filled pastries.

**picadillo:** A meat dish similar to hash.

**plantains:** Large green bananas that are used like vegetables.

**ropa vieja:** A meat stew that looks like shredded bits of cloth.

**saffron:** An expensive yellow-orange spice.

**sautéing:** Frying lightly and quickly.

**simmer:** To cook slowly over low heat.

**sofrito:** A mixture of onions, bell peppers, and garlic that is the basis for many Cuban dishes.

**tasajo:** Dried meat similar to beef jerky.

**tenderizes:** Makes softer.

**tostones:** Twice-fried plantains.

**tres leches cake:** A rich cake moistened by three kinds of milk.

**yuca:** A tough root vegetable that softens when it is boiled. It is also referred to as cassava or manioc.

## Books

Alison Behnke, *Cooking the Cuban Way*. Minneapolis: Lerner Books, 2004. A Cuban cookbook for kids.

Richard A. Crooker, *Cuba*. New York: Chelsea House, 2010. Looks at Cuba's geography, history, government, economics, and culture with maps.

Sandy Donovan, *Teens in Cuba*. Mankato, MN: Compass Point, 2008. Looks at the daily lives of teenagers in Cuba.

Roger Hernandez, *Cuba*. Broomall, PA: Mason Crest, 2009. Discusses Cuba's economics, history, culture, and geography with lots of color pictures.

## Web Sites

**National Geographic Kids**, "Cuba," (http://kids. nationalgeographic.com/Places/Find/Cuba). Offers facts, great photos, a video, a map, and an e-card.

**Taste of Cuba** (www.tasteofcuba.com/index.html). A Web site with many Cuban recipes and photos of Havana.

**U.S. Central Intelligence Agency: The World Fact Book**, "Cuba," (www.cia.gov/library/publications/

the-world-factbook/geos/cu.html). Gives information on the Cuban people, government, geography, economics, military, and challenges the nation faces. Includes a map and a flag.

# Index

# Picture credits

## About the Author

Barbara Sheen is the author of more than 50 books for young people. She lives in New Mexico with her family. In her spare time she likes to swim, walk, garden, and read. Of course, she loves to cook!